# Welcome, Stranger:
## Poems of Making and
## Keeping Our Children

*poems by*

# Melissa Weaver

*Finishing Line Press*
Georgetown, Kentucky

# Welcome, Stranger:
## Poems of Making and
## Keeping Our Children

## ACKNOWLEDGMENTS

"Alchemy" first appeared in *The Christian Century*, March 2017
"Song and Shuttle" first appeared in *Mothers Always Write*, April 2017
"Consolation" first appeared in *Mothers Always Write*, September 2017
"Like Fine Red Veins" first appeared in *Anabaptist Witness*, October 2017
"I Cannot Hear of Bees" first appeared in *Mothers Always Write*, August 2018
"Blue Heat" first appeared in *Mothers Always Write*, August 2019
"Manna" first appeared in *Bravery Magazine*, Issue 10, February 2020

Publisher: Leah Huete de Maines
Editor: Christen Kincaid
Cover Art: Julia Morrell
Author Photo: Patrick Weaver
Cover Design: Elizabeth Maines McCleavy


Order online: www.finishinglinepress.com
also available on amazon.com

Author inquiries and mail orders:
Finishing Line Press
PO Box 1626
Georgetown, Kentucky 40324
USA

# Table of Contents

*To the Father who made a place for me at His table.*
*To the firm grip on my hand at the kitchen table.*
*To those we have welcomed.*
*You are our great wonder, joy, and aching love.*

## A Beginning

His match
strikes soft,
this fusion
fuse-lit
amidst (against?)
the unknown
darkness. Sparks
fly fast
along the path
that's carved into the image
I bear. An explosion.
Communion keg of dew on backs of Adam and Eve
(pre-tree) leaves
our throats
with breaths
like smoke.
We fade,
but in our breaking,
there's
an ember.

## Welcome, Stranger

Make yourself
at home. I'll be your host,
most days, most gracious.
Put your feet up
on my bladder one more time, though,
and I'll need my security back.
(Good for you, eviction
is a rather painful process).
Please, *mi cuerpo es tu casa,*
but you'll have to forgive
our dust. These renovations
are messier
than we expected.

## I Cannot Hear of Bees

I cannot hear of bees, bombs
dropping like driving rain

that will drown, rocks that will cry out,
one-in-three and M-16s,

every inclination in a stranger or
in me. My ears, my door are shut

from the outside for 40
weeks, just the two of us amid creaks and groans.

You will rock inside my waters until
ready, Dove, you'll leave me.

Then, I will attend to mud
and bones and altar stones
again.

## Trimester Three

If I didn't think I'd break
it, I'd find a desk somewhere,

take a load off and let
a lesson begin:

"This was our known world.
You can see now how everything

has shifted." I've got a meridian now,
new tributaries, too, that I'm afraid won't fade

despite all of South America's
best buttered intentions.

Your continent feet rise and
sink like Atlantis,

history changed with what goes
on under my surface.

**5:06 AM**


I am wishing
for a more poetic
memory than five
red neon characters
on a white-washed
O.R. wall.

## Valentine's Day, 2015

It must have been the pineapple juice,
sipped through wide straws, spicy salsa,
or His timing,
or neither,
or both,
but you came:
month early
mirror of the blizzard
beyond our windowpanes
bursting
into light, tearing me
but somehow not your skin
the thickness of tissue paper.

Hello, Little Pilgrim, drink.
Your travels were winding.
here is where we start
walking together.

## Blue Heat (Third)


We knew you'd be electric.
The air was pregnant with pause.

We rocked and waited,
sweating through the summer,

thought the thunder too far
or not coming.

White-laced clouds gathered
and we counted down

rumbles and rain,
the rising and the cresting and

the dissipating pain.
We didn't know your weight

could dislodge,
trace from arms
to brain, veins constricting

until lightning
made us learn to walk again.

Six weeks 'til our smiles
could rise to even.

## Nursing, Two Days After Two

Let me remember this:
your hand on my shoulder
slides under my shirt sleeve,
and I am silk.
I am quilt.
I am tonic and
Cream.

**Dry Season**

Early spring parenting:
*All* the bodily fluids
but what started this.

## Brave Little

This world has stones,
and I am no giant.

It has lips parched,
and I cannot squeeze

hard enough for water.
I can only hope

the Tailor ever more
skilled than I

can make my whey enough
to whet your voice

for crying out
in deserts.

## Song and Shuttle


Let this lullaby loose what slipped
through the thick cord as you spun
and were spun in my dark belly room.

May the waves from my lips
shake your dry bones ear-hid
'til the double-strands
we've handed down Pattern fit.

Come, *Cantus Firmus,*
reverse weft, hidden warp,
rework fruit dripping

down
and down
dark 'simmon red.

**Baby Meets a Burning Bush**


Your first forsythia flames lemon-yellow,
branches wrapped in stars split wide
from Warm Breath brushed so near.

May you always reach for trumpets
telling us this ground is holy,
leave your sandals off despite
the plastic bags rolled near your feet.

May you see a tabernacle
where they see a park pavilion,
find the Blaze that bestows glory
in the faces that you meet.

**Spitting Image**

Exhibit A of Dark and Bright,
are these elusive patterned pairs a Jacob's ladder
or a dark descent?

What is hairline
cracks in chromosomes
and what spirits sewn into the lining of seeds?

Mess and Marvel,
how do we begin to trace the lines
of curse and grace and

freckles, Cupid's bow, face
in certain light?
How do we manage to measure

not just places where our minds
pool in greasy back-alleys
but the same way our words

dart like dragonflies,
the way that we sing
up at trees?

**10:16 PM**


The three of you
are in cahoots. A musical
fountain of screams
requires at least light collaboration.
Your beds must be molten
or your pajamas laced with shards
of sugar. You insist
it's your doll's daytime.
New incisors make a titanic dent
in your dreams. It's a Wednesday.
Whatever the case, I've ruled
the flood God innocent, regretting
what He'd made.

**4:30 AM**


Maybe because you're a strange blend
of both of our flesh, our scents,
neither of us notice when you slip
in between us,
again, under cover
of night and plenty of sleep
deprivation. And when
we wake with two feet
in our faces and much less
on our sides, we still can't hide
wonder at eyelashes,
and lungs and lengths of rib bones.
You are three feet of eminent domain
in footed pajamas;
we don't even protest.
You, who lay claim to where
we once lay down in your making,
go
ahead, take us. We're
yours.

## Manna

We're in wilderness now, you and I,
some days wandering, lips white
with rage; the world's spread too wide.

Your dewy baby curves are
gone, replaced by sturdy body,
limbs like bread I gather every night
to rock when all grows cool.

Honey, sometimes you bewilder me
with what you are but (wonder!)
you are wafer on my tongue.

After all, I had wanted out of Egypt.

**Icons**

Their bottoms are my abbey bells,
their coughs my calls to prayer
3   6   9   12   3
And baby teeth become rosary beads,
relic locks of hair are slipped
into envelopes, pressed
against our lips in this,
no ordinary time.
Whines pour and my white flesh is laid
on a lapping tongue,
echo of Eucharist
Here
amid liturgy of bread
                brush
                backpack
                bus
                *(Have mercy on us, Lord!)*
Someone must sit for Madonna,
Lap full, full of grace.
It might as well be
Weary, willing
Me.

## Preload

There are days I want to bolt,
you drive me nuts,
the way you spin
around my soul. I'm stretched, hung
by a thread, the friction
in my head, breasts, heart,
too much, our days compressed
by mess and moan and growing
pains. And yet—
this constant press, holds
us, against all odds, at odds,
together.

## Alchemy

Your black moods, chaos— I'm at a nonplus.
There's no panacea for tiny flying fists.
I want your life to deny what dust
we are. His

transformation is not gnosis
but my white knuckles have no trust.
They want to squeeze the base from you (I wish it were more noble),
dismiss

mortality, immaturity, Rose-Dawn on each of us.
From this day's ashes, revelation—no "golden child" but instead this:
You are not my *magnum opus.*
We are His.

**Mama!**


I am vessel waiting in the wings at Cana:
you pull and my blood blooms into what you love best.

I am desert oil: explosions, factions flare
when my well dares to dry.

In your cupped hands, I'm Helen's
water: splash and recognition as a stroked and sifted stream,

a genie three tiny masters wake with kisses,
despite a thousand and one sleepless nights.

I am guide in this jungle: just as lost as you find yourselves,
with a few more slips of map clutched in my fingers.

## Consolation

Ballerinas' toes are black.

Thorns of lead lace rose-
window tracery.

Marie's bones burned
from laughing long days
in potato-shed/stable,
Radium salt glowing by her bedside—
and they called her Nobel.

My grandfather baptized
bursts of hands and light and strung
immortal moments in dark clouds
of Sulphur-dioxide.

I think of this when my knees prick
with crumbs and my thumbs wrinkle
like a kitchen-sink Sisyphus.

When I get on eye-level
to find what fell
from a diaper, I swear

there must be a sonnet
in here somewhere.

**Everyday, Used**


The ants go marching one by one, across
the kitchen floor that wishes for the past
feet of childless vegan owners, whose dross
was always organic. It groans at last

night's "dino-nugget" carnage, stubs our toes
to spite us for the times we turned our back
on full-moons waxing wildly while the clothes
dried, rises in odd spots, avenging cracks.

But not the walls. They shiver with delight
as hands trace down their lengths and galleries
appear with robots AND Snow White. New heights
rise on their ribs and T-Rex shadows tease

a singing puppet queen. Both wood, both scarred,
but that which welcomes life, bears weight, wears art.

## Synonym Cycle

Girl—
Hummingbird, maker, conductor, song;
I'm wonderstruck the whole day long.

Boy—
Tumble, trip, grin, flash,
Magnet eyes and constant crash.

Hers—
Scribbled poem of her devotion,
beads strung, hands in constant motion.

His—
Muddy lips, smashed weed-flower
Again! Again! Again! (An hour)

Mine—
Thick, surprising, in my chest
Waved ambition finally crests.

## Metaphors

My late-summer rattle of morning-glory globes
twisted on the porch rail:

vines on a temple somewhere
ruled by monkeys climbing rotting stones.

or, a withered life spent
after a long summer-time of giving.

To you: "A swing
for Jesus. '*Whee*! I'm up in heaven!
I am up in heaven
with the little children.'"

# Trinity Playground, Advent 2014

*or a toddler teaches on Isaiah 11*


We are people who put stock in seeds,
bellies swollen with sure leaves,
expiration dates stamped on their packets' neat seams.

You are furrowed brow,
unsteady legs on rocked playground,
bending, scattering fistfuls of sawdust   in   breeze.

You sow, laughing lithe prophet,
a pageant, a rumor: shoots that spring up
from slivers, the ashes of trees.

## Home-video Harbingers

*"Then Elijah said to Ahab,*
*"Go get something to eat and drink,*
*for I hear a mighty rainstorm coming!"*
*—1 Kings 18:41*


Seven days slipping on the steamy cement
of a roof in monsoon rains,
bare-bellied prophets break from books and laps to
sway in the sea-
sweat of hand-clouds and
thunder claps.
   The word of the Lord
    to brick roofs:
        oil still swirls inside thick clay,
        outstretched bodies still breathe
        life into dead,
        shoulders brush yet past hot flanks,
        droughts will still yield
        to bent heads.

## A Single Drop

Some will say it's swept away (gravity
and all that). But what if

for the joy of River's dance it chooses desert—
losing self to flow

in water that's untold millennia old? With millions
faithful, further up (or down?) and further in,

unaware, it carves a canyon,
nations drawn to its great rim.

## Like Fine Red Veins

Like fine red veins in yolk, these bends
pulse so you'll grow,
lithe and reaching.

These turns burn: more like buried
than burrowing, head-against-stones in the dark,
hard, blind weaving.

But beneath honeycomb graves there are rumors of Water
that will run through our cells, roll down
sweet mighty stream.

I'll keep twisting deep, sink, come and drink
of the mystery; you'll spread, mirror of seeking,
as you gulp light, bear,
leave.

## Anatomy of an Arrow

*"Subordinate to the bow, its charismatic companion,*
*but purposeful in its intent, the arrow epitomizes*
*both silent death and joyous recreation."*
*–Hugh D.H. Soar, Straight and True:*
*A Select History of the Arrow*


God's gift to Adam, martyrs' scepter, released
stored energy in flight,
shaft of light with hard spine,
flint head turned toward distant target.

Story: energy in flight,
Three fletches steady a
flint head turned toward distant target,
a body marked as Archer's, for His aim.

Three fletches steady a
shaft of light, hard spine of
body marked as Archer's. For his aim,
God's gift to Adam, martyrs' scepter, now
released.

Melissa Weaver lives in Harrisonburg, Virginia, where she tends to a steady husband, three small children, a growing watercolor illustration business, an unruly backyard garden and occasionally, a poem or two. She writes about motherhood and faith, identity and legacy, and the intersection of the surprisingly sacred and mundane. She is particularly interested in the beauty, fragility and connection that emerges in the act of radical hospitality that is parenting. A former English/ELL teacher, she seeks to be deeply rooted in her diverse neighborhood, building relationships with kids and families from all over the world. Her work has appeared in *The Christian Century*, *Bravery Magazine*, *Mothers Always Write*, *Anabaptist Witness*, *The Anabaptist Journal of Australia and New Zealand*, and *Transforming*, a publication of Virginia Mennonite Missions.

CPSIA information can be obtained
at www.ICGtesting.com
Printed in the USA
JSHW020916290121
11287JS00001B/18